30 Days of Encouragement

# POWER
# UP!

FAITH HOPE TRUST

VOL. 2

## Erraldo L. Budhan

EMI

Extra Mile Innovators
Kingston, Jamaica

. . . . .

Published by
Extra MILE Innovators
54 Montgomery Avenue, Kingston 10, Jamaica W.I.
www.extramileja.com
ruthtaylor@extramileja.com

Editor: Carlene Dacres

Book Cover Design:
Christopher Lawrence and Amoy A. Lawrence,
The Anointed Writer | logomepleasejm@gmail.com

Cover Retrofitting: Pro-designer Olivia

**Author Contact**

For Conferences, Workshops, Crusades, Conventions, Seminars, Youth Ministry Development Consultation contact Erraldo Budhan by email at elbministry@gmail.com.

# NOTES

*To my young brothers: D'Jean and ReJean Budhan*
*I try my very best to be an inspiration and a role*
*model to both of you.*

# YOUTH REVIEWS

The book *Power Up Vol. 1* is simply authentic. Not only are you being encouraged daily but you are given the opportunity to express yourself with the activities provided. The author shares experiences which helped me to relate and comprehend the encouragements received daily. Vol 1 of *Power Up* has helped me to grow spiritually as an individual and it has helped me to keep track of my progress and prayers. I am excited about Vol 2 based on the power imparted from Vol 1. I would recommend this book to everyone because this book has definitely helped me to Power Up."

—Ja-Donne Gray
Church of God of Prophecy, Long Hill

•   •   •   •   •

*Power Up Vol. 1* was published at the right time where I had to make some very important decisions in life concerning my future. Its publication came at a time where I wanted evidence for what I have been praying about; evidence and testimonies. I am looking forward to Vol. 2 because volume one has impacted my life greatly.

—Samuel Cummings
Church of God of Prophecy, 41 Old Harbour Road

•　•　•　•　•

*Power Up Vol. 1* was exactly what I needed, especially with what I've been going through and the questions that came to my mind concerning God's integrity; questioning God's integrity. *Power Up Vol. 1* motivated me to keep going even when I wanted to stop. Reading the testimonies encouraged me to trust God more. My faith, hope and trust have gotten stronger, and I am more secure in my Christian walk, knowing that God is able to give me what He has promised me. I still re-read Vol. 1 up to this day and now I am excited to read Vol. 2. I encourage everyone to invest in this book for themselves or for someone else.

—Shaquille Hall
Touch Me Faith Deliverance Ministries

•　•　•　•　•

*Power Up Volume One* was an extraordinary read. It taught me to pencil down the things I desire from God while providing encouraging testimonies. I think as believers we should invest in our development and growth so that we can function in the capacity that God purposed for us. *Power Up* has definitely facilitated that growth and I would love for you to get an encounter too. Get a copy and catapult into the original version of who God has called you to be. I await the release of Volume 2.

—Vonorica Throught
Praise Sanctuary
Church of God of Prophecy, Cavaliers

# INTRODUCTION

Life comes with challenges and in all things, we are encouraged to take on life's challenges head on and win. Each day you will be encouraged to do great, be great, experience great things and reflect on the greatness of Jehovah God. I beseech you therefore, brethren, by the mercies of God: READ AND BE GREAT!

I assume you have already read the first thirty (30) days of encouragement in Volume 1. *Power Up* started out as one big book but the recommendation to break up the book in parts was an ingenious idea because the encouragements are much easier to digest and reflect on. Volume one was intense and Volume 2 is no different. It is designed to build your faith, hope and trust.

The storms of life come to make us and never to break us. You can only be broken and torn up in the storms if your anchor is not gripped firmly to Jesus Christ. *Power Up* is designed to expel fear and doubt from our lives and plant seeds of faith, hope and trust in God.

Volume 2 of *Power Up* continues to pour encouragement into the heart, mind and soul of those who read it. Every text given is an encouragement explained and made applicable to this contemporary era. You will be able to apply each encouragement and text to your life, see God work and see your faith grow. Each encouragement carries a reflection. The reflection is to see the encouragement activated in your life. After the reflection, you are encouraged to write a declaration in the book for each day.

# TABLE OF CONTENTS

# Day 1
## TRUST GOD AS YOUR KEEPER

"The Lord keeps you from all harm and watches over your life" (Psalms 121:7 NLT).

I n the text above David alluded to God as his keeper. We are encouraged to trust and believe that God will keep us in and through the seasons of life.

## Encouragement

David encouraged himself in more ways than one. He reminded himself that his help came from God. He also reminded himself that God does not slumber nor sleep. God is always watching and when God watches, God keeps. He is wide awake and He has His hands on you. You have to learn to trust God. Believe that He will keep you during your exile season.

Some of us have been there before. You may have been in your own Babylonian exile experience but rest assured that God keeps. Know that God also protects. This protection is not a one-off or for a season but God's protection is forever. The Lord sleeps not. And He does not hesitate to rescue us from the midst of the struggle. Trust the keeping God. I am assured that God will keep and deliver you from whatever Babylonian experience you may be in. Just encourage yourself by knowing that God is keeping you.

## Testimony

In a season of my life, I felt as if I was going to backslide. I'm a church boy. I grew up in church and got saved at age 14. In that season of my life, I felt like I was in exile. I was ready to let go until I remembered where my help came from. God kept me when I felt like going astray. To date, I stand to say I'm kept by the keeping God and I believe He will never let me go. Today, trust God to keep you.

**I beseech you therefore, brethren by the mercies of God: Trust God to keep you.**

In this season, you may experience exile but trust that God will keep you alive in it all.

# Brawta Scripture

"Now all glory to God, who is able to keep you from falling away and will bring you with great joy into his glorious presence without a single fault" (Jude 1:24 NLT).

# REFLECTION

Do you feel kept by God?

_____

_____

_____

_____

_____

_____

Where in exile are you?

_____

_____

_____

_____

_____

I encourage you to trust God to keep you in this season.

# Write to God

# DAY 2
# GIVE THANKS UNTO THE LORD

"Give thanks to the Lord, for he is good! His faithful love endures forever" (Psalms 107:1 NLT).

## Encouragement

The text above encourages us to give God thanks all the time. God has been so good that we must give Him thanks. David starts Psalm 106 and 107 using the same liturgical doxology. If you missed it in Psalm 106, you will definitely find the opening again in 107. There are two fundamental reasons why we must give God thanks. The reasons expressed in the Psalms are this: first, we must give God thanks because He is good.

Look back over your life and think on every good thing that God has done for you. If you should put pen to paper to record these good deeds the Lord has done, you would be writing an endless paper. I assure you, there are many good things that have happened in your life, and all good things come from the Father.

The goodness of God is sometimes unexplainable and even undeserved. He still shows us love and kindness. We are encouraged to give Him thanks because He is good. The Psalmist did not give us a past tense of the goodness of God nor did he give us the future. He gives us a present tense that we can use every day. Each morning you wake up, **God is good;** each evening you close your eyes, **God is good**.

The second reason we are encouraged to give God thanks is that *His love endures forever.* Sometimes we get to a point in our lives where we feel unloved. It is at that time we must remember that God's love abounds and it abounds forever. Loneliness is a serious issue. I have always heard the saying and even experienced it before, "that you can be lonely while surrounded by others." When we experience loneliness, we must rest assure that the love of God is around us to embrace us, and this love endures forever.

# Testimony

I experienced the always present goodness and love of God in my life during my final year of college. Please note, I have always experienced the goodness and abounding love of God but this time stood out for me. I was finishing up my final year and months before graduation, I applied to Gordon Conwell Theological Seminary (GCTS) to do a dual master's degree program: Master in Divinity (M.Div) and Mental Health Counselling (M.H.C). Months passed, and I did not get a response.

Finally, I received an email saying I had gotten preliminary acceptance into the M.Div programme but had to reapply to gain admission into the M.H.C programme. I was excited because now I had the opportunity to study overseas. But I had just started attending my new church, Life Centre Tabernacle Church of God of Prophecy, and I felt sad at the fact that I would have to leave for three years to study abroad.

Although I was happy, I did not get the chance to follow through with the study due to financial reasons. I thought that everything was just no longer working in my favour. I then applied to a school in Jamaica, the Caribbean Graduate School of Theology, and I got accepted immediately to do the Master of Arts in Theological Studies.

I started giving God thanks because I recognized that the Lord had shown me that I had what it takes to study abroad and in my own country. The goodness of God amazed me because GCTS sent me an email yearly to inform me that my admission is being waived until I am ready to study there. God is good and I give him thanks.

**I beseech you brethren by the mercies of God: Give thanks unto the Lord.**

There must be something good to give God thanks for today. What is it that you can think of? When you think about it, give Him thanks because He is good. His love is abounding and endures forever.

## Brawta Scripture

"I will praise you, LORD, with all my heart; I will tell of all the marvelous things you have done" (Psalm 9:1, NLT).

# REFLECTION

Think about three good things the Lord has done for you.

How do you feel?

_____

_____

_____

_____

_____

_____

_____

_____

_____

How do you respond to the goodness of God?

_____

_____

_____

_____

_____

Let's talk to God.

# Write to God

_____

_____

_____

_____

_____

_____

_____

_____

_____

# Day 3
# KNOW JESUS FOR YOURSELF

When Jesus came to the region of Caesarea Philippi, He questioned His disciples: "Who do people say the Son of Man is?" They replied, "Some say John the Baptist; others say Elijah; and still others, Jeremiah or one of the prophets." "But what about you?" Jesus asked. "Who do you say I am?" Simon Peter answered, "You are the Christ, the Son of the living God." Jesus replied, "Blessed are you, Simon son of Jonah! For this was not revealed to you by flesh and blood, but by My Father in heaven. And I tell you that you are Peter, and on this rock, I will build My church, and the gates of Hades will not prevail against it. I will give you the keys of the kingdom of heaven. Whatever you bind on earth will be bound in heaven, and whatever you loose on earth will be loosed in heaven." Then He admonished the disciples not to tell anyone that He was the Christ (Matthew 16:13-16, BSB).

The text above tells us of the conversation between Jesus and His followers when He asked them: "Who do men say I am?" The text en-

POWER UP VOL. 2

courages us to know Jesus for ourselves.

## Encouragement

I strongly believe that for us to know ourselves we must first come into a relationship with God. We must have a revelatory experience of who Jesus is in order for us to know who we are. Our true identity is found in God. Genesis says it all, that we are made in *His image*. It is not possible for someone to profess Jesus without first knowing Him personally. For you to profess Christ, you must have an intimate relationship with Him. Many persons know of Christ but do not really know Him. There is victory in knowing Jesus and knowing Him means to believe in and on Him.

Jesus asked the disciples two simple questions when they had come to Caesarea Philippi. The first question was: "Who do men say I am?" That question was then followed by "Who do you say I am?" The disciples answered the first question but only one of the many could have answered the second question accurately. Peter answered the second question by saying: "You are the Christ, the Son of the living God." It is in this text that Jesus called Peter, "rock." In our journey of life, we must be able to give an answer when the question arises, who is Jesus to you? Our answer should not be what others are saying but it should be what we know for ourselves. I encourage you to know Christ for yourself just as Peter did.

## Testimony

I was in a store giving out some brochures for my undergraduate college, Jamaica Theological Seminary, when an atheist walked in. I was in my second year of study and had just started majoring in Theology. I was telling the store clerk about Jesus and the atheist got upset, and started to speak negatively about Christianity and exclaimed that "there was no God." It dawned on me then, that we are going to encounter hurting persons in the world who will deny Christ because of how they feel. I turned to the atheist and I said: "Jesus loves you."

I was not about to debate the existence of God but I just wanted her, the atheist, to know that although she did not believe in God at the moment, God still loved her. It was my experience of knowing Christ why I could calmly turn to her and express that truth with such boldness. When you know God for yourself, you will not be afraid to share His love with others.

**I beseech you brethren, by the mercies of God: Know Christ for yourself.**

Do not depend on the testimonies of others to get you through this life. Build your testimony by building a strong relationship with God.

## Brawta Scripture

"But grow in the grace and knowledge of our Lord and Savior Jesus Christ. To him be glory both now and forever! Amen" (2nd Peter 3:18, NIV).

# REFLECTION

Who do men say Jesus is?

_____

_____

_____

_____

_____

Who is Jesus to you?

_____

_____

_____

_____

_____

_____

_____

_____

Do you have a personal relationship with Him?

_____

_____

_____

_____

_____

_____

Let's talk to God.

## Write relationship goals with Christ.

_____

_____

_____

_____

_____

_____

_____

_____

# Day 4
## APPRECIATE YOUR VALLEY EXPERIENCE

The Lord is my shepherd;
I have all that I need.
He lets me rest in green meadows;
he leads me beside peaceful streams.
He renews my strength.
He guides me along right paths,
bringing honor to his name.
Even when I walk
through the darkest valley,
I will not be afraid,
for you are close beside me.
Your rod and your staff
protect and comfort me.
You prepare a feast for me
in the presence of my enemies.
You honor me by anointing my head with oil.
My cup overflows with blessings.
Surely your goodness and unfailing love will pursue me
all the days of my life,

and I will live in the house of the Lord
forever (Psalm 23:1-6, NLT).

The text tells us of David traversing through the valley on his way to Jerusalem. He had to face the Philistines but assured himself that God was with him. We are encouraged to appreciate the valley experiences in our lives.

## Encouragement

As Christians, we are faced with the circumstantial situation of journeying through some gloomy moments in our life. The Christian faith is not easy but it is certainly worth it. On our journey, we must be mindful that before we get to the mountain we have to go through the valley. And for some, this valley can be called *The Shadow of Death*. In order for us to appreciate the mountains, we must first appreciate the shadow of death experience. The valley experience is set to humble us and to make us into better individuals. We must not regret the valley or curse it but we must appreciate it. It is the valley that we trod to get to the mountain.

Whenever we are facing a valley experience, we must be reminded that the valley is not the final stop. Never get disappointed in the valley, but be encouraged that in the valley, God is with you. To appreciate this valley experience, we must know who is shepherding us. David declared that God was his shepherd and therefore he would not lack anything. Who shepherds you? In every valley experience, God has a way of relaxing time and keeping you safe. David experienced this when he said that the Lord led him beside still waters and into green pastures. In this valley experience, you may face enemies but rest assured, God is with you. Though you go through the 'shadow of death,' nothing can harm you. Be encouraged today to appreciate your valley experience because it is preparing you for greater things.

## Testimony

This testimony comes directly from the text. David is journeying back to Jerusalem and has to go through the valley. In the valley, there were ravines and along these ravines lived the Philistines. David knew this and declared that he would not be afraid. This experience helped David to trust God more and rest in the serenity of God. We see this when David declares that God is with him. He passed through the valley and reached his destination safely. David sat as king in Israel. The valley was just for a season.

**I beseech you, therefore, brethren, by the mercies of God: Appreciate the valley.**

The valley experience is just for a season. In the valley, you will learn to trust God more and you will also see the hand of God working miracles in your life. Your experiences build character. The valley experience will build a "mountain" character.

## Brawta Scripture

"God is our refuge and strength, always ready to help in times of trouble" (Psalm 46:1, NLT).

# REFLECTION

What valley experience are you facing?

_____

_____

_____

_____

_____

_____

_____

_____

What are you afraid of?

_____

_____

_____

_____

_____

_____

Who is shepherding you?

_____

_____

_____

_____

_____

Let's talk to God.

# Write to God

About your valley experience.

_____

_____

_____

_____

# Day 5
## TRUST GOD EVEN WHEN YOU CANNOT FIND HIM

Then Job spoke again:
'My complaint today is still a bitter one,
and I try hard not to groan aloud.
If only I knew where to find God,
I would go to his court.
I would lay out my case
and present my arguments.
Then I would listen to his reply
and understand what he says to me.
Would he use his great power to argue with me?
No, he would give me a fair hearing.
Honest people can reason with him,
so I would be forever acquitted by my judge.
I go east, but he is not there.
I go west, but I cannot find him.
I do not see him in the north, for he is hidden.
I look to the south, but he is concealed.
But he knows where I am going.
And when he tests me, I will come out as pure as gold.

For I have stayed on God's paths;
I have followed his ways and not turned aside.
I have not departed from his commands,
but have treasured his words more than daily food'
(Job 23:1-12).

This story tells us of Job's search for God and his resolute decision to trust God even when God couldn't be found. We are encouraged to trust God even when God goes silent.

## Encouragement

I remember preaching this sermon the first time: "What happens when you cannot find God?" I have preached that sermon at least four times, and every time I preach it, I am reduced to tears. Job experienced a season of silence in his life and this silence was coming from God. Job had been through much and had lost much. He lost his earnings, his children, his wife and his health. The enemy requested permission from God to perplex Job in order to prove to God that Job would deny Him. Job had it all and the Bible said that he avoided sin, and yet God gave the enemy permission.

I have always heard sermons from the book of Job and the question is always asked, "Can God recommend you to be tempted of the devil?" The question is asked so that we can look into our lives to see if we are really living for God well enough for God to brag and boast about us. God could brag about Job; therefore, God gave the enemy permission to afflict him.

From chapter one through to chapter 23 where we are, throughout Job's troubles he did not hear the voice of God. God had gone silent. I believe that God seemingly deserts us so that our faith in God can be strengthened. There are going to be times when we will not hear from God, feel Him, or sense a move from God. When the time comes, what will you do? What happens if God should choose to step back and go silent for even a month, would you reconsider trusting God?

The story of Job ended with God doubling all that Job had. In the season of God's silence, God was still with Job. He still trusted God even though he could not find Him. Although God went silent, He was still there. I encourage you to trust God even when He goes silent. At the end of the silence, God will have a blessing awaiting you.

## Testimony

God went silent on me before. I appreciated it later because it helped to build my faith. I prayed to the Lord to kill a struggle in my life, and each time I prayed the struggle got harder. I could not hear the voice of God. I felt as if I was lost without any hope of being found. In the midst of the silence, I decided to trust God. Then a shift happened in my life, and I finally got a word. The word that broke the silence was "NO." At that point, I wish God had remained silent because that was not the word I wanted. Today, I appreciate both the silence and the response from God. My life is far better now than it was before. It was like Job's case when God responded. God asked Job some strong questions. I, too, had questions asked of me, and then I was encouraged that even when God is silent, He is working in my life.

**I beseech you therefore, brethren, by the mercies of God: Trust God even when you cannot find Him.**

God's silence does not mean that He is not present and standing beside you. Trust Him even when you cannot find, see or hear Him.

## Brawta Scripture

"As for God, his way is perfect: The LORD's word is flawless; he shields all who take refuge in him" (Psalm 18:30, NIV).

# REFLECTION

In which season have you experienced the silence of God?

_____

_____

_____

_____

_____

_____

How did you feel?

_____

_____

_____

_____

_____

_____

How did you react?

_____

_____

_____

_____

Let's talk to God about it.

# Write to God

How do you feel when you think God has gone silent?

_____

_____

_____

_____

_____

_____

_____

Write to yourself about why you should trust God during the Divine silence.

_____

_____

_____

_____

_____

# Day 6
## BE TRANSFORMED!

"Don't copy the behavior and customs of this world, but let God transform you into a new person by changing the way you think. Then you will learn to know God's will for you, which is good and pleasing and perfect" (Romans 12:2, NLT).

We are encouraged in the text to present our bodies to God and be transformed by renewing our mind.

## Encouragement

"Be ye transformed by the renewing of your mind," is a powerful charge, telling us that we must go through spiritual metamorphism to clear our minds from things that do not give glory to God. The expression means we must change our habits and form and put on another form or adopt another habit that will reflect the glory of God in our lives. We are not encouraged to change our wardrobe or hairstyle but we are encouraged to change that innate persona that does not reflect the glory of God.

Transformation comes through renewal, and renewal only happens through the power of the Holy Spirit. Our views and feelings on things must change once we enter into the process of mind renewal and transformation. Transformation starts from the mind and for many of us, the mind is like a battlefield. The word "mind" is applicable to the whole spirit distinguished from the body including the understanding, will and affections.

Therefore, the change and transformational experience should not be apparent to the body only, but also to the soul. If the mind does not change then all external changes would not be useful. For us to be transformed, we must first submit to God. After submission, we must let the Holy Spirit renew our entire being and after that renewal, we must walk in the good and acceptable will of God. Today, we are encouraged to go through a spiritual renewal in order to experience a great transformation.

# Testimony

I have always been hard and fast when making decisions and to be honest, most of the time I believe I am right. However, a point in time came when my philosophy was challenged, and it was challenged for my good. I was placed in a position to think not just with my intellect but on a spiritual level. My mind was greatly influenced by my knowledge of psychology, and my behaviour was coming off as arrogant and obnoxious. I failed to see the truth presented to me until I had prayed and asked the Lord to open my spiritual eyes and give me a heart and mind like Christ.

After that prayer, I was able to see what was being explained to me. I experienced a mind renewal and those around me saw the change in my behaviour. It was a transformational experience. I believe that for true transformation to take place, we must pray to God to renew our mind.

**I beseech you therefore, brethren, by the mercies of God: Be transformed and live renewed.**

Try and see things from another perspective. Ask the Holy Spirit to renew your mind so you can think with the mind of Christ and act accordingly.

## Brawta Scripture

"This means that anyone who belongs to Christ has become a new person. The old life is gone; a new life has begun!" (2nd Corinthian 5:17, NLT)

# REFLECTION

What aspect of your life do you want the Lord to transform?

_____

_____

_____

_____

Have you asked the Holy Spirit to renew your mind?

_____

_____

_____

_____

_____

Are you struggling with submission to God?

_____

_____

_____

_____

_____

Have you completely sacrificed your life to God?

_____

_____

_____

_____

_____

_____

Let's talk to God.

# Write to God

_____

_____

_____

_____

_____

_____

_____

_____

_____

# Day 7
## YOU ARE LOVED!

"For God loved the world so much that he gave his
one and only Son, so that everyone who believes in
him will not perish but have eternal life"
(John 3:16).

The text above epitomizes God's love for all of
us. Be encouraged, you are loved by the Creator.

## Encouragement

At times we may feel as if we are unloved and unwanted. Love is defined in so many ways by people all over
the world. Some believe that love is when you wait up
for them until they get home at nights. Others may be-

lieve that love is when they get a text from a special person in the morning as they rise. Some believe that love is attached to financial gains and exchanges. We all have a definition of love but the best definition of love is the **agape love.** It is seen in how God shows us how important we are to Him.

The first human beings disregarded the laws of God and sinned against God causing destruction to come to humanity. We were no longer in the Garden talking with God in the cool of the day, but now we are outside clothed in a sinful state wondering if there is the hope of ever returning to Eden where we once were. Even in our sinful state, God loved us so much that He made a huge sacrifice.

Many parents would never even consider giving up their only child to die for others but God gave His only begotten son for you and me, so that we could once again commune with Him as we did in the Garden of Eden. We are so loved that God did not banish us

and send us into oblivion but washed away the stains of sin and took us into His arms. Whenever you feel unloved and underappreciated, remember that the Creator loves with you as a good father loves his child.

## Testimony

I was raised in a wonderful home where my family showered me with love. I never experienced the feeling of being unwanted or unloved. Yet although I was shown love, at some point in my life, I felt like I needed reassurance that I was loved and that I was important. The Holy Spirit reminded me of the golden text of the Bible: **John 3:16.** I am forever reminded, even when I don't feel it that I am loved by Almighty God and that has kept me happy ever since. My parents and family love me and I am grateful for that but the fact that God loves me more, makes me even more excited. I encourage you today my readers, to know that you are loved by God.

**I beseech you therefore, brethren, by the mercies of God: Never forget that God is in love with you.**

If no one else shows you unconditional love, remember this, God's love for you will never change.

## Brawta Scripture

"But God showed his great love for us by sending Christ to die for us while we were still sinners" (Romans 5:8, NLT).

# REFLECTION

Do you feel unloved?

_____

_____

_____

_____

_____

_____

How do you express love to others?

_____

_____

_____

_____

_____

_____

Have you ever questioned God's love for you?

_____

_____

_____

_____

Let's talk to God.

# Write to God

How do you feel about God's love for you?

_____

# Day 8
# THINK POSITIVELY

"And now, dear brothers and sisters, one final thing. Fix your thoughts on what is true, and honorable, and right, and pure, and lovely, and admirable. Think about things that are excellent and worthy of praise" (Philippians 4:8, NLT).

## Encouragement

The mind is a powerful thing. This is where our creativity begins. For those of us who are not impulsive, everything we do we first think long and hard about it. We apply the steps involved in the decision-making process and explore the possible outcomes of certain actions. We also look at the effects these decisions may have on our lives. At the end of the day, we assure ourselves that we thought about it before we did anything. We are encouraged to think on positive things; things that will uplift and build us. We should never sit down and think on the negativities of life and let them weigh us down, but focus our mind on the things that are true about us in the eyes of God. Think about the things that are pure and right for us. If we start thinking positively, then we will live more productive and happier lives. Think positive things concerning you. Start thinking positively today.

## Testimony

Having started college in 2012, I began 'thinking big.' I was majoring in Guidance and Counselling until one of my favourite lecturers and head of the faculty for Theology, Rev. Barry Hall suggested that I change my major to theology. He said, "That is where you belong." I made the switch in my second year and my big thinking got bigger. Before, I saw myself as a Counselling Psychologist but in changing my major, I changed my thinking and began to see myself as a Theologian, a Pastor and a Clinical Psychologist.

I thought long and hard about how I would achieve those goals. With hard thinking comes writing, believing and praying which you will be encouraged to do in subsequent days. I made sure that my actions were in line with my big positive thinking. Today, I am a thinker and a doer. I've experienced it. Once you think it, then you can achieve it. Think big today. Think Positive.

**I beseech you therefore, brethren, by the mercies of God: Think positively about things concerning you.**

Never linger in the rivers of negativity. The plan of God for your life is for you to be great. Start thinking long and hard on the positives and see how your life will change for the better.

## Brawta Scripture

"Think about the things of heaven, not the things of earth" (Colossians 3:2, NLT).

# REFLECTION

What positive thoughts do you have for yourself?

_____

_____

_____

_____

_____

_____

What big thing are you thinking about that will impact your life positively?

_____

_____

_____

_____

_____

_____

_____

Let's talk to God.

# Write to God

Tell Him about your big plans

_____

_____

_____

_____

_____

_____

_____

_____

_____

_____

_____

_____

_____

# Day 9
## WRITE IT

"This is what the LORD, the God of Israel, says:
'Write in a book all the words I have spoken to you'"
(Jeremiah 30:2, NIV).

## Encouragement

Writing is not easy. I can attest to this because this little encouragement guide that you are reading, came to me when I decided I was going to write whatever the Lord said or had revealed to me, but I found it was easier said than done. God has deposited in some of us a passion for writing and for some He has shared with them visions and dreams. Even if you are not a writer, it is good to keep records of the words that God has given you. This record is something you can go back and re-read. Write down the visions that you have gotten. Dreams that you have dreamt, write them down. Inspirational thoughts that come to your mind, write them down. It is always good to have a writing pad near you so that whenever things pop up you can record it.

God told Habakkuk to write the vision so that the ones who will read it will run with it. Someone is waiting for you to write your vision. It may not be elaborate as you expected it to be, but it is something someone is waiting on. Writing takes time, dedication and drive. You may have started writing and have given up. God may have placed a book in you and all you need to do is write. Do not let fear stop you from writing what God has for you to do. Write as you know it. In creating goals, we are encouraged to write because writing makes it stick. Today, I encourage you to write even the things you do not understand. God will give you the interpretation later when you are ready for it, but for now, just write.

## Testimony

I was telling a very good friend of mine that I should have never paused from writing. It was the most difficult thing to resume. I had the ideas in my head but I had gotten too lazy and started to find countless excuses as to why I had to put it off until the following day. After almost one week of being on a break, I kept on hearing in my spirit that someone out there was waiting to be encouraged and I was being lazy. During my little break, the Lord gave me a topic, "You Can Still Colour," and I wrote it down and went back to being "tired."

I finally awoke from the slum of laziness and began writing. I started writing everything I heard in my head. These very words you are reading were not premeditated or from an outline, this was me listening and writing. I am a preacher by calling and never saw myself in the world of authors but this time I decided, if the Lord wants me to write then I will write. You are now reading the result of what God encouraged me to do.

**I beseech you therefore, brethren, by the mercies of God: Write the vision plain as you get it.**

A friend of mine often gets dreams and visions. Some she really doesn't understand and neither do I. I encourage her that whenever she gets a vision, a dream or something comes to mind, just write them down. Have a book called "Visions and Dreams" and write as you see and hear. Write the vision as plain as you get it.

## Brawta Scripture

It said, "Write in a book everything you see and send it to the seven churches in the cities of Ephesus, Smyrna, Pergamum, Thyatira, Sardis, Philadelphia, and Laodicea" (Revelation 1:11, NLT).

# REFLECTION

Have you dreamt any dreams?

_____

_____

_____

_____

_____

_____

Have you seen any visions?

_____

_____

_____

_____

_____

How do you record your deepest thoughts and your most passionate inspiration?

_____

_____

_____

_____

_____

Do you think writing down your visions, thoughts and passions will help you to keep proper records?

_____

_____

_____

_____

_____

_____

Let's talk to God

## Write to God

_____

_____

_____

_____

_____

_____

_____

# Day 10
## BELIVE IT

"If you believe, you will receive whatever you ask for in prayer" (Matthew 21:22, NIV).

## Encouragement

Think it. Write it. Believe it. It sounds simple and yes, it really is. You have thought of all the big plans God has for you, and you have received the visions and dreams concerning your life, now you just need to believe it. At this stage, people's faith gets shaky because believing is hard. It is hard to believe when nothing seems to be working out. You thought about it and you wrote it down, but nothing is working out as you expected it, so how then can you believe?

Believing God for what He has for you comes through faith. If you have faith, you will receive. Belief and faith go hand in hand. The big plans you have, believe that they will happen. It may not happen when you want it, and probably it may not come the way you expect it, but if you have faith in God, then your belief is not in vain.

Believe the vision, the dreams and the big plans that God has for you. Believe even in the midst of uncertainty. Believe in the midst of the darkness that there is light at the end of the tunnel. Believe that you are greater than how you see yourself. Today, I encourage you to believe!

## Testimony

I studied counselling in college and an older student expressed that young people, like myself, should not study counselling because no one would listen. I disregarded every word she said in that class, and I made it my duty to put her words to shame. I told myself, "you are going to do great in the counselling arena," and I **believed it.** I write to you to say I have served two institutions as a Guidance Counsellor and the last educational institution where I worked, the principal said I came highly recommended to the school. I worked at both institutions and left a positive mark on teachers, parents, staff and students. I believed the plan of God for me. I have had good experiences in counselling and I still believe God for the big things that I am thinking about.

**I beseech you therefore, brethren, by the mercies of God: Believe God in all you do.**

Never be daunted by delays in life, but be encouraged by the unwavering word of God that says the plans God has for you is great. Believe, if only on this one thing: *God has big plans for you.*

## Brawta Scripture

"Faith is the confidence that what we hope for will actually happen; it gives us assurance about things we cannot see" (Hebrews 11:1, NLT).

# REFLECTION

What are you believing God to do?

_____

_____

_____

_____

_____

_____

What has God told you about that you need to believe?

_____

_____

_____

_____

_____

_____

When you believe, you will receive. Let's talk to God.

# Write to God

Write about His promises to you.

_____

_____

_____

_____

_____

_____

_____

_____

_____

_____

_____

_____

_____

_____

_____

# Day 11
# FAITH IT AND RECEIVE IT

"Until now you have not asked for anything in my
name. Ask and you will receive, and your joy will
be complete"
(John 16:24, NIV).

Before receiving, we have to ask. At the beginning of our 30 days encouragement, we beseeched you to ASK God for all that you want. Asking + Seeking + Knocking = ASK. The first step to receiving comes from asking. We asked, then thought about it, wrote it down, believed what we asked for, now it is time for us to receive it. If we never ask, we will never receive, but if we ask all things in the name of Jesus, then so shall we receive all that He has for us.

Receiving is the fruit of your petition. When the Lord blesses you, that means you receive what you asked for, and sometimes you receive blessings for which you may not have even asked. Not only should you just receive it, but "faith it." This means we must act as if we have it before we actually get it.

Sometimes we won't get it right away, but we must faith it nonetheless, until we see the manifestation of God's word in our lives. Act like you know it. Act like you have it. You might think that's crazy but it's a faith move. *Faith it* until you receive it. If you wish to be a great preacher, teacher, singer, banker etc., act like you are until God calls you to that office or post. If your faith is weak, you won't receive. So today, I encourage you to *faith it* until you receive it.

## Testimony

I've always wanted to be a Bishop in the Lord's church. I strongly believe I am called to pastoral ministry. I see myself as an Apostle planting and growing churches through the power of the Holy Ghost. When I got convicted of this, my entire way of life changed. I started to act like the role I wished to attain.

My walk and even my talk became different. I walked with authority and humility at the same time. I interacted with people and showed my love for people.

I was "faithing it" and I am still "faithing it" until the Lord finally appoints me to serve in that office.

Today, I serve as a youth minister in my church organization as a Parish Youth Director. I supervise the youth ministries of 39 churches with the responsibility of growing the ministry and conducting workshops, seminars, retreats and other events that will impact the lives of youths. I am getting close to the office of an Apostle. I can taste it. I'm "faithing it" as God teaches me all I need to know. *Faith it* until you receive it.

**I beseech you therefore, brethren, by the mercies of God: Faith it until you receive it:**

I was reading *Purpose Has No Shame* by Leroy Hutchinson and he cited TD. Jakes saying, "Fake it until you make it." It was from *Purpose Has No Shame* I borrowed the words "Faith It." You are not faking what God has called you to do. You are moving by faith into it. And remember, faith is something you can't see but something you hope for.

## Brawta Scripture

"Whatever you do, work at it with all your heart, as working for the Lord, not for human masters, since you know that you will receive an inheritance from the Lord as a reward. It is the Lord Christ you are serving" (Colossians 3:23-24, NIV).

# REFLECTION

What have you asked for?

_____

_____

_____

_____

_____

What have you thought about?

_____

_____

_____

_____

_____

Have you started to *faith it*?

_____

_____

_____

_____

_____

Do you believe that you will receive it?

_____

_____

_____

_____

_____

Let's talk to God.

## Write to God about your 'faithing it' experience.

_____

_____

_____

_____

_____

_____

_____

_____

_____

# Day 12
## BE IT

All the tribes of Israel came to David at Hebron and said, 'We are your own flesh and blood. In the past, while Saul was king over us, you were the one who led Israel on their military campaigns. And the LORD said to you, 'You will shepherd my people Israel, and you will become their ruler.' When all the elders of Israel had come to King David at Hebron, the king made a covenant with them at Hebron before the LORD, and they anointed David king over Israel. David was thirty years old when he became king, and he reigned forty years. In Hebron, he reigned over Judah seven years and six months, and in Jerusalem, he reigned over all Israel and Judah thirty-three years (2 Samuel 5:1-5, NIV).

## Encouragement

Interestingly, when we have "faithed it" (acted it), and received it, we are now commissioned and encouraged to be it. Be who God has called you to be, and be it without fear. David was anointed as King but he didn't become king until the time was right. Right timing is in the eyes of God, and when the time is right God will reveal it to you. David defeated Goliath with the anointing of a king but he was not in the office. He "faithed it" until he received it.

When David finally became king, he became that for which he was training. Some of us have to go through training in order for us to fully appreciate what God has called us to be, and for us to actually be the best version of ourselves. If you believe God has given you what you asked for, and you truly believe you have received this, be it. Let no one stop you from being who God has called you to be. Faith it. Receive it. Now BE IT.

## Testimony

I started working in media as a relief broadcaster. I always wanted to be a media personality. When I was hired as a relief, I acted as if I was a main broadcaster. I went on air and when covering someone's shift I did it to the best of my ability. I 'faithed it' until finally I was promoted to being one of the main broadcasters for the radio station. I worked the afternoon shift which was considered a hard shift because the listenership at that time is very high and even companies listen to the programme.

I told myself at that time, "Whenever you go into the studio and turn on the microphone, speak to Jamaica and the world. You must be great." BE IT and you will do great. Be who God has called you to be. Be you and be great.

**I beseech you therefore, brethren, by the mercies of God: BE IT!**

Never be scared of what God has called you to be or where God has called you. Step up to the plate and be it and be it well.

## Brawta Scripture

"So, God created man in his own image, in the image of God he created him; male and female he created them" (Genesis 1:27, ESV).

# REFLECTION

Who has God called you to be?

_____

_____

_____

_____

_____

_____

How are you trying to be this person?

_____

_____

_____

_____

_____

_____

_____

_____

Where do you see yourself in five years?

_____

_____

_____

_____

_____

_____

Let's talk to God.

## Write to God

Tell God about the process of being who He has called you to be.

_____

_____

_____

_____

_____

_____

# Day 13
## PURSUE IT

"Depart from evil and do good; Seek peace and pursue it" (Psalm 34:14, NASB).

## Encouragement

Pursuing something or someone relentlessly means to do it without the intention of giving up. In volume one of *Power Up*, we were encouraged to not quit—to not give up. In this volume, the opposite of giving up is **pursuit.** Just like God relentlessly pursues us to save us from the darkness of the world, so too must we relentlessly pursue Him, and the things of His kingdom. Seek it and pursue it.

An army that is on a mission to retrieve a fallen soldier caught in the land of the enemy does their utmost best to seek the best route to take to invade the enemy's territory. After successfully finding and explaining the process of evacuation, they start to pursue. Fervently, they arm themselves and relentlessly traverse the terrain until they reached their desired destination to retrieve their fallen comrade. Just like an army, we must have our goals in mind, seek after it and pursue it relentlessly. It is in purview. Can you see it? Can you feel it? Well, if you can then go ahead and pursue it. Pursue what God has laid up in storage for you. Pursue what is yours but may be held in captivity. Pursue relentlessly!

## Testimony

If you are reading this book in 2020, I want to inform you that I am currently in pursuit mode. I'm pursuing a Master of Arts Degree in Theological Studies. I often felt like giving up because of some courses I did and would encounter in the future. I felt some courses were going to get the best of me. I met some courses that I had done in the undergraduate program that I did not think would meet me again. But whenever I feel like giving up, I remind myself of the goal ahead.

The goal is to get that Ph.D. under my belt and in order to do so, I have to pursue and then conquer. I can only reach the conquering stage if I pursue. I completed one semester already and I'm heading into another. Writing this book has been helping me to practise writing a much longer thesis. In this season, I am relentlessly pursuing my goals and I encourage you to pursue yours.

**I beseech you therefore, brethren, by the mercies of God: Pursue them relentlessly.**

Seek after what you need from God, and pursue Him for it relentlessly.

## Brawta Scripture

"Seek the Kingdom of God above all else, and live righteously, and he will give you everything you need" (Matthew 6:33, NLT).

# REFLECTION

What are you seeking God for?

_____

_____

_____

_____

_____

Are you relentless in your pursuit?

_____

_____

_____

_____

_____

Do you have a timeframe on when you want it?

_____

_____

_____

_____

_____

_____

Let's talk to God:

# Write to God

Tell Him about what you are pursuing.

_____

_____

_____

_____

_____

_____

# Day 14
# CONQUER IT

"But in all these things we overwhelmingly conquer
through Him
who loved us" (Romans 3:37, NSAB).

## Encouragement

Y ou are more than a conqueror. I am certain
you have heard that phrase before and it is a
much-quoted by Christians worldwide. This
Scripture is a reality. As believers, we are more than
conquerors. In the New Testament, we are told that we
have overcome the world because Jesus has overcome
the world. It is time we live the life of victors and not
victims. It is time we live like winners and not losers.
Losing is not acceptable. This does not mean that we
will not fail at some things, but it means we will not

accept the failure and call it quits. We all have something that we want to attain, although some of us have pushed it to the back of our minds. We have something that we want to master and something that we want to rule over. Joshua in the Old Testament was commissioned and instructed by God to take Jericho which had been promised to them.

In that time, Jericho had an almost impenetrable wall as a deterrent to outsiders. The inhabitants of Jericho were not going to let anyone take their land and so Joshua sent spies to assess the land. After receiving the updates on the land, Joshua and his team decided that they were going to pursue and conquer. The walls of that city were torn down by the power of Almighty God. Joshua and the Israelites went over and conquered. Whatever is standing in your way, I encourage you to conquer it. Let the walls in your life know that you will not give up. You will fight and pursue until the walls fall because at the end of the day you must come out more than a conqueror.

## Testimony

The first time I went on air as a broadcaster, I was extremely nervous. I had no words in my head and I was shaking like a leaf during a storm. It was a Saturday morning and I was assigned to the broadcaster in the studio who would monitor an outside broadcast. The General Manager was working and her shift was coming to an end. She saw how nervous I was, sat with me and talked me through the first half hour. I sounded nervous. I sounded and felt as if I was going to choke on almost every word that came out of my mouth.

Back then, I was just a relief announcer. I did not have a programme for myself. I completed the shift; it wasn't perfect but I completed it. I got more experience working on the early morning shift called "Love in the Morning." I decided that I would become good at this. I put Philippians 4:13 (I can do all things through Him who strengthens me) to good use and talked myself through it. I must conquer the fear. I must speak with great boldness.

Today, I am the main broadcaster for the afternoon programme and the Saturday morning programme on LOVE 101 FM. I conquered the fear and thanks be to God, now I am doing extremely well. In my efforts to continue winning, I enrolled in a course on Oral Fluency in order to become a master in this field. Today, I encourage you, be the conqueror and not the conquered.

**I beseech you therefore, brethren, by the mercies of God: Do not let it conquer you but conquer it.**

Whatever stands in your way, remind it and yourself that you are more than a conqueror and you will stand above it and never beneath.

## Brawta Scripture

"No, despite all these things, overwhelming victory is ours through Christ, who loved us"
(Romans 8:37, NLT).

# REFLECTION

What do you want to conquer?

_____

_____

_____

_____

_____

What plan have you put in place to conquer it?

_____

_____

_____

_____

_____

_____

_____

Do you see yourself as a conqueror?

_____

_____

_____

_____

_____

# Write to God

About the walls that are before you

_____

_____

_____

_____

_____

_____

_____

_____

# Day 15
# POSSESS IT

"Be strong and courageous, for you are the one
who will lead these people to possess all the land I
swore to their ancestors I would give them" (Joshua
1:6, NLT).

## Encouragement

God has promised you the land, now it is time to possess it. The story of Joshua is one of the best foundational stories we can look at in relation to possessing what is ours. God promised Moses the land but it was left to Joshua to lead Israel to the point of possessing it. On Day 14, we looked at how Joshua sent spies into the land to assess the land. We also mentioned that the wall of Jericho fell before their eyes, and they then went in and killed all those who needed to die, so they could be the conquerors. After conquering the enemy who had their possession, Joshua and the nation of Israel stood up as the rightful owners of the land which was given to them as their possession. We have to be determined to conquer and possess.

Many of us have seen the walls fall before our eyes, we have destroyed the enemies in our lives but we have yet to possess what is really ours. Why are you looking at the possession but afraid to take it? It is yours. God has given it to you and once God has given a thing to you, no one can take it away from you. You need to develop boldness and take hold of the gift that God has given to you and use it. You have conquered and today God is telling you, possess it. The giants have all been killed and the treasure is waiting for you to take it and walk away with it. You are the rightful owner. Today, I encourage you to possess your possession.

## Testimony

When I served as a Guidance Counsellor at a school in Kingston, Jamaica, I was teaching a class and had to confiscate a student's phone, because one of the rules of the school states, "No phone should be seen or heard." After confiscating the phone, I took it to the Vice Principal's office and the rightful owner had to be the one to retrieve it. It so happened that I was at the Principal's office at the end of the school day when a student came requesting the phone. However, that student was not the rightful owner. Therefore, the phone could not be handed over to the student.

I commissioned the student to find the rightful owner and have that student come to the office with an ID to retrieve the phone. A few minutes later, the student came and apologized for her insubordination to the rules of the school and the phone was returned to her. She was elated! Normally, if she had sent someone else, the phone would have been locked away and she would have to pick it up another day. Only the rightful owner can possess what is theirs. Today, I encourage you, as the rightful owner, possess what is yours.

**I beseech you therefore, brethren, by the mercies of God: Go and possess it!**

A popular Jamaican saying goes like this: *What is fi yuh cannot be unfi yuh.* In other words, if it is yours it cannot be anyone else's.

## Brawta Scripture

"I promise you what I promised Moses: 'Wherever you set foot, you will be on land I have given you" (Joshua 1:3, NLT).

# REFLECTION

What do you want to possess?

_____

_____

Are you going after it?

Do you see yourself with it?

## Write to God

Tell Him the dreams and aspirations that you want to possess.

_____

_____

_____

_____

_____

_____

_____

_____

_____

_____

_____

_____

_____

_____

# Day 16
# BE AUDACIOUS

Leaving that place, Jesus withdrew to the district of Tyre and Sidon. And a Canaanite woman from that region came to Him, crying out, "Lord, Son of David, have mercy on me! My daughter is miserably possessed by a demon." But Jesus did not answer a word. So His disciples came and urged Him, "Send her away, for she keeps crying out after us." He answered, "I was sent only to the lost sheep of the house of Israel." The woman came and knelt before him. "Lord, help me!" she said. But Jesus replied, "It is not right to take the children's bread and toss it to the dogs."

"Yes, Lord," she said, "even the dogs eat the crumbs that fall from their master's table." "O woman," Jesus answered, "your faith is great! Let it be done for you as you desire." And her daughter was healed from that very hour (Matthew 15:21-28, NLT).

# Encouragement

To be "audacious" means to be bold, fearless and in some regards, it could mean to be stubborn. In reading a book written by Valentine Rodney titled *Shameless Persistence,* he encourages us to be bold in our approach to God. To be "audacious" means you will not relent but you will persist until you get what you require. If shame is in your game, then audacity is not in your capacity.

To be audacious, you have to be shameless. You cannot be easily intimidated and easily offended if you really want something. You must be bold. We have heard it more than once in this encouragement guide: we must be bold in all that we are doing. God is looking for audacious people to approach Him without shame.

Have the audacity to tell God your mind. He already knows what you are thinking, you need to be honest with yourself and honest with Him and just tell Him.

In encouraging some of my young people to pray more, I tell them to be real with God. Tell Him everything. Whether you are disappointed in how He did something or whether you are elated. Let someone say: "How dare you?" and just respond, 'I have the audacity to talk to God." Audacity does not mean disrespect and by no means should we approach God with disrespect, but it means to be bold and approach God with a relentless spirit.

# Testimony

I had a big issue and God seemed to not have cared much concerning it. I developed this relentless spirit to challenge God because I felt as if He was ignoring me. I went boldly before His throne in prayer night and day about the issue. I became audacious and relentless and demanded of God, in the most respectful way, an answer. After days, weeks and even a couple months, God responded to me with Scripture.

I was not happy with the response but I was comforted that He was hearing me and that He answered. There was no shame in my game. I became audacious and talked to God as if I had no other choice because honestly, I had no other choice. Today, I am grateful that I developed the spirit of audacity because now I can rightfully go boldly before the throne of grace and make my petitions known, relentlessly. I encourage you to have the audacity!

**I beseech you therefore, brethren, by the mercies of God: Be audacious!**

It is best to be stubborn and bold than to be stubborn and weak. Go to God with an audacious spirit and persist in prayer until He has no choice but to respond to you.

## Brawta Scripture

"So, let us come boldly to the throne of our gracious God. There we will receive His mercy, and we will find grace to help us when we need it most" (Hebrews 4:16, NLT).

# REFLECTION

Can you approach God boldly?

_____

_____

_____

_____

_____

When last have you poured out to God in prayer?

_____

_____

_____

_____

_____

_____

_____

Do you think being audacious in prayer is important?

_____

_____

_____

_____

## Write to God

Tell Him your request and be audacious about it.

_____

_____

_____

_____

_____

_____

_____

_____

_____

# Day 17
## GET UP

Peter and John went to the Temple one afternoon
to take part in the three o'clock prayer service. As
they approached the Temple, a man lame from
birth was being carried in. Each day he was put beside the Temple gate, the one called the Beautiful
Gate, so he could beg from the people going into
the Temple. When he saw Peter and John about to
enter, he asked them for some money. Peter and
John looked at him intently, and Peter said, "Look
at us!" The lame man looked at them eagerly, expecting some money. But Peter said, "I don't have
any silver or gold for you. But I'll give you what I
have. In the name of Jesus Christ the Nazarene get
up and walk!" (Acts 3:1-6, NLT)

## Encouragement

How long have you been settling with the
worries and pressures of life? Today it is
time to get up. In most of the New Testament miracles, the person receiving the healing or de-

107

liverance is encouraged to get up and walk or to "go thy way." Like the man at Gate Beautiful, many of us are waiting on someone to hand us something that can change our lives miraculously. We have been sitting and waiting on something to happen and finally, God sends the right person, the right word, the right prophecy, the right encouragement but it needs the right response. Our response to God's word is very important.

Many times, we pray to God and He gives us an answer, but our response was either been delayed or we had no response at all. The man at Gate Beautiful saw Peter and John and asked them for money because he thought that was what he needed. Just like you and me, there are times we have in our minds an image of what we think is needed for the specific moment, but God has in His plans what is needed for our entire life to be right. The man asked for money but the apostles instead gave him a command; the command was "to get up." They denied him what he wanted but gave him exactly what he needed. He wanted money but he desperately needed healing.

Today God is giving us exactly what we need and the command to see the manifestation of it is "to get up." Get up out of depression and you will see and experience happiness. Get up out of worry and you will experience peace. Get up out of laziness and you will see the manifestation of good works in your life. The man got up by faith and he started walking. I encourage you to get up and start walking into the manifestation of God's will for your life.

# Testimony

I was praying to the Lord for financial breakthroughs to take care of my loans and the Lord gave me a command. It was to do His work. I have a passion for church growth. My 9-5 job did not give me the time to plan and do what God wanted me to do. Therefore, I resigned from my desk job at the end of 2018. I got up in 2019 with the plans for church growth on my mind. Like the beggar, God did the opposite of what I wanted. I wanted money, but all He gave me was work. After resigning, I started worrying about paying my car note and my school fee.

The Lord reminded me that a minister was going to help with my school fee. Soon after, I went to preach at a retreat and I was blessed financially with the necessary cash to pay my car note. After this, I went to a conference in St. Kitts and Nevis, in that same month of January, without paying any money for my flight. I also stayed at a hotel in St. Kitts and Nevis without going into my pocket. I got up and God did the rest.

**I beseech you therefore, brethren, by the mercies of God: Get up!**

Getting up requires faith but it also requires action. Today, get up from where you are and do what God called you to do.

## Brawta Scripture

Sometime later there was a feast of the Jews, and Jesus went up to Jerusalem. Now there is in Jerusalem near the Sheep Gate a pool with five covered colonnades, which in Aramaic is called Bethesda. On these walkways lay a great number of the sick, the blind, the lame, and the paralyzed. One man there had been an invalid for thirty-eight years. When Jesus saw him lying there and realized that he had spent a long time in this condition, He asked him, "Do you want to get well?"

"Sir," the invalid replied, "I have no one to help me into the pool when the water is stirred. While I am on my way, someone else goes in before me." Then Jesus told him, "Get up, pick up your mat, and walk." Immediately the man was made well, and he picked up his mat and began to walk" (John 5:1-9, NLT).

# REFLECTION

What are you sitting down thinking about?

_____

_____

_____

_____

_____

_____

_____

Why haven't you moved as yet?

_____

_____

_____

_____

_____

_____

Will you take action today?

_____

_____

_____

_____

_____

_____

## Write to God

Tell Him about your future moves?

# Day 18
# BE PERSISTENT

When they reached Jericho, and as Jesus and his disciples left town, a large crowd followed him. A blind beggar named Bartimaeus (son of Timaeus) was sitting beside the road. When Bartimaeus heard that Jesus of Nazareth was nearby, he began to shout, "Jesus, Son of David, have mercy on me!

Be quiet!" Many of the people yelled at him. But he only shouted louder, "Son of David, have mercy on me!" When Jesus heard him, he stopped and said, "Tell him to come here." So they called the blind man. "Cheer up," they said. "Come on, he's calling you!" Bartimaeus threw aside his coat, jumped up, and came to Jesus.

"What do you want me to do for you?" Jesus asked. "My Rabbi" the blind man said, "I want to see!" And Jesus said to him, "Go, for your faith has healed you." Instantly the man could see, and he followed Jesus down the road (Mark 10, 46-52, NLT).

## Encouragement

D ay 18 sounds like we are repeating our-selves. We have already been encouraged to not quit, to conquer and to be bold. It seems as if all those are the same as being persistent. If you were thinking that you are right but I wanted to illus-trate persistence through the beautiful story of blind Bartimaeus. Persistence is key to getting what you want. Blind Bartimaeus needed healing. He wanted his sight. Jesus was passing by with a crowd of onlookers and the blind man cried out. In his cry to Jesus, he was addressed by a few members of the crowd that told him to be quiet.

The blind man was not about to let powerless nega-tive people stop him from getting what he wanted so he became bold, audacious and persisted in calling out to Jesus. Because of his persistence Jesus responded and gave him what he asked for. Never let anyone or anything to stop you from getting to your destination or getting what you want. Be persistent until you get it. The first shout might not yield the results you want, but be persistent in doing what is good and noble in the eyes of God, until you get an answer. Your persistence will attract the attention of Jesus.

## Testimony

Sometimes persistence can be seen as annoying. I have been annoyed before and I have also been a source of annoyance to others. I have an aunt who shows persistence until she annoys me. She was literally days away from flying to the United States and she persisted in calling me almost three times a day for about three days (prior to her leaving) asking me to take her to the airport before daybreak. I kept on saying "no" because it would mean that I had to get up too early and then go to a full day of work. She persisted in calling and asking until she simply wore me down and I consented. Needless to say, she was elated. I took her to the airport because her persistence annoyed me to a point where I felt I had to consent. May you be persistent enough to annoy God until He responds to your cry. Like Jacob, don't let go until He blesses you.

**I beseech you therefore, brethren, by the mercies of God: Be persistent!**

Be determined and be deliberate!

## Brawta Scripture

Then the man said, "Let me go, for the dawn is breaking!" But Jacob said, "I will not let you go unless you bless me." (Genesis 32:26, NLT).

# REFLECTION

What are you persistent about?

_____

_____

_____

_____

_____

_____

How do you see persistence in your spiritual life?

_____

_____

_____

_____

_____

_____

Are you being deliberate in getting what you want from God?

_____

_____

_____

## Write to God

Ask God to help you to persist amidst the odds of life.

_____

_____

_____

# Day 19
# BE POSITIONED

Jehoshaphat was terrified by this news and begged
the Lord for guidance. He also ordered everyone in
Judah to begin fasting. So people from all the
towns of Judah came to Jerusalem to seek the
Lord's help" (2 Chronicles 20:3-4, NLT).

## Encouragement

Posture and position in life are very important.
Your posture says it all and so, too, your position. In Jamaica, people will look at your posture to surmise your behaviour or your upbringing. I
was always told to sit up straight and walk upright because that would indicate that you are ready to go and
not slump around. Your position can somewhat predict
your future experiences and challenges. The story of

Jehoshaphat is an interesting one to use to talk about being in the right position at the right time.

We are encouraged in this passage to position ourselves and watch the Lord fight the battles in our lives. In order for the Lord to fight these battles, we have to position ourselves to be still and watch. Day 19 is the introduction of three positions I want us to take as we build our faith, hope and trust in God. In the subsequent days, we will examine the position of prayer, the position of obedience and the position of worship. Today, as we get ready to position ourselves, I encourage you to make sure that your position in life is rooted in God.

## Testimony

I am very much Jamaican but as it relates to sports, you will only find me excited when it is Olympics season. During the Olympics, my favourite sport to watch is track and field. If we examine the runners well, they have been trained for the task and when they get to the starting line, they fall into what they believe is the best posture or position to run.

Usain Bolt, the famous Jamaican runner, as fast as he is, will ensure that his starting position is excellent. Whenever you look closely at the races, you will find that the person whose starting position was flawed may not win the race or may struggle to stay in the race to win first, second or third place. It is always the one who positions well and puts in enough training that will succeed. I pray we get our starting position correct as we run the race of life.

**I beseech you therefore, brethren, by the mercies of God: Be positioned for what God wants to do in your life.**

Sit up straight, walk upright, look ahead, speak properly, smile and make sure your posture and position reflect that of a winner.

## Brawta Scripture

"But Moses told the people, "Don't be afraid. Just stand still and watch the LORD rescue you today. The Egyptians you see today will never be seen again" (Exodus 14:13, NLT).

# REFLECTION

What starting position are you in?

_____

_____

_____

_____

_____

How effective is your current posture in life?

_____

_____

_____

_____

_____

Is the position you are in correlating to the position
God wants you in?

_____

_____

_____

_____

_____

_____

_____

_____

# Write to God

Tell God about your current positions.

_____

_____

_____

_____

# Day 20
# POSITIONED IN PRAYER

Jehoshaphat stood before the community of Judah
and Jerusalem in front of the new courtyard at the
Temple of the Lord. He prayed, 'O Lord, God of
our ancestors, you alone are the God who is in
heaven. You are the ruler of all the kingdoms of
the earth. You are powerful and mighty; no one
can stand against you! O our God, did you not
drive out those who lived in this land when your
people Israel arrived? And did you not give this
land forever to the descendants of your friend
Abraham.

Your people settled here and built this Temple
to honor your name. They said, 'Whenever we are
faced with any calamity such as war, plague, or famine, we can come to stand in your presence before
this Temple where your name is honored. We can
cry out to you to save us, and you will hear us and
rescue us.'

And now see what the armies of Ammon, Mo-
ab, and Mount Seir are doing. You would not let
our ancestors invade those nations when Israel left
Egypt, so they went around them and did not de-
stroy them.

Now, see how they reward us! For they have come to throw us out of your land, which you gave us as an inheritance. O our God, won't you stop them? We are powerless against this mighty army that is about to attack us. We do not know what to do, but we are looking to you for help (2 Chronicles 20:5-12, NLT).

## Encouragement

You can never talk too much about prayer, and I know that you have encountered prayer in this book before. It is through prayer that we tell God what's on our heart. Today, I want us to look at the intentional way of praying. Prayer as we know it is communication between man and God. Sometimes when we pray, God does not respond audibly. It does not mean that He does not hear us, it could mean that His answer can be sought in the holy book called the Bible.

In our attempt to get into the right position we must be able to go to God with our deepest grouses and praises. Prayer is about emptying ourselves at the feet of the Father. Jehoshaphat heard that the armies from the surrounding nations were coming to attack Judah and he became scared. Just like many of us, situations arise in our lives that sometimes cause us to be fearful.

Out of fear, Jehoshaphat prayed. He brought his grouses to God and basically asked God if He (God) would let the other nations defeat him. Jehoshaphat did not think it was enough for him to be the only one to talk to God, so he commissioned the people of Judah to pray and fast.

A life of prayer is important because it is through prayer, we will get divine strategies from God to assist us on the journey of life. You will never know the heart and will of God unless you are positioned in prayer. Prayer is key and today I encourage you to position yourself in prayer and listen for instructions from the Lord.

## Testimony

Prayer and fasting have been a struggle for me. I am a good preacher who loves reading the Word of God, but I realized that my prayer and fasting life was not where it ought to be. I needed more from God and could only get it if I denied myself and sought Him in prayer. It was time for classes to begin again and I was ready to sit out another semester because of financial challenges. I prayed earnestly and humbly asked God to find a way for me to start the actual master's programme and not sit out the semester. Through prayer, I was prompted in my spirit to email the school to ask if I could start a course without doing certain prerequisites, knowing I had an unpaid balance.

I emailed the school, and they instructed me to email my professor and academic dean. I did so and prayed for favour. The Lord did grant me favour. I got consent to do two courses without first doing the prerequisites. As simple as it probably sounds, for me my Master of Arts in Theology programme is extremely important. Every day I sought God for help because I still did not know how I was going to pay for my courses.

One Sunday morning, I led worship and after completing worship at church, a minister pulled me aside and asked me about school. I told her of the challenges and she said to me, "I'll pay for one of your courses." I was beyond elated and started giving God thanks. Through prayer, I learned that God expects us to ask anything of Him. I hope that you will be encouraged to position yourself in prayer.

**I beseech you therefore, brethren, by the mercies of God: Position your ears to the mouth of God—Pray.**

Pray more, listen more, read more and again, pray, pray, pray! It is best to talk to God about everything than to not talk to Him at all.

## Brawta Scripture

"In my distress I prayed to the LORD, and the LORD answered me and set me free" (Psalm 118:5, NLT).

# REFLECTION

Do you see prayer as a challenge?

_____

_____

How often do you pray?

Do you pray in your own authentic way?

Before we talk to God, let me suggest a prayer cycle that probably can work for you.

## Prayer Cycle

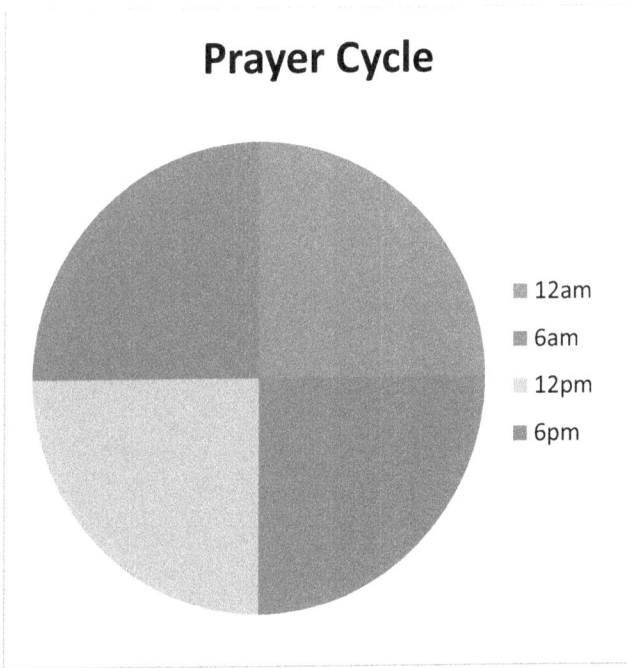

- 12am
- 6am
- 12pm
- 6pm

## Pray around the clock

Following this prayer cycle, you do not need to pray long; all you need to do is just say a few words to God from your heart. There are four quarters set as examples. You can identify your most suitable prayer time, and just design your own cycle, set your alarms or reminders and just talk to God at those designated times.

This does not eliminate spontaneous praying, but it will keep you on track to commune constantly with God.

Use the sample prayer cycle below as a guide and create your prayer cycle. Then record your prayer cycle.

## Write Your Prayer Cycle to God

_____

_____

_____

_____

_____

_____

_____

_____

_____

_____

_____

# Day 21
# POSITIONED IN OBEDIENCE

"But you will not even need to fight. Take your positions; then stand still and watch the Lord's victory. He is with you, O people of Judah and Jerusalem. Do not be afraid or discouraged. Go out against them tomorrow, for the Lord is with you" (2 Chronicles 20:17, NLT)!

## Encouragement

In a Caribbean culture, it is rough not to be obedient. Obedience is the very best key to prosper in life and in God. Lack of obedience can cause our lives to be chaotic and filled with disasters. To have a life controlled by the will and power of God, we must be obedient to God. The humanity of our being will push us at some point to be disobedient, and that is because obedience sometimes seems like the hardest thing to do. Some instructions given seem ridiculous, and to obey seems like a burden at times. We are faced in life with obstacles, and God gives us instructions daily; we get our instructions from the sacred text and through prayer. Whenever we go to church or a gathering where the Word of God is spoken in our hearing, we must get a command or instruction, and we must obey such in order to see the manifestation of God's providence for our lives.

Jehoshaphat heard of the impending war upon Judah, and he consulted God. He poured out his heart to God because he did not know what else to do. While Jehoshaphat was pouring out his heart to God, God sent an instruction through Jehaziel saying that Jehoshaphat must go out on the mountain and watch the Lord fight the battle. Out of obedience, Jehoshaphat went out with the people of Judah and they watched the word of the Lord come to pass.

What battle are you currently in, and what instructions have you gotten from God? I encourage you to be obedient even if the instructions given seem ridiculous. God's ways are higher than the ways of men; all we need to do is obey Him and He will take care of us.

# Testimony

Sometimes God will give us instructions that sound ridiculous. I was preaching at a church in the parish of St. Ann, and during the altar call segment, the Lord told me that He would be healing people. Even though I prayed for signs and wonders to follow my ministry, I was scared to say that God was going to perform healing. A few friends came with me, and one looked at me, without me telling her anything, she said: "Do it, say it."

I then called persons up for prayer and prayed with them for the Lord to heal them in whatever area they needed healing. One person had a problem with her feet, and I heard the Lord telling me to have the lady stand on both my feet. I was hesitant because this seemed a bit unorthodox.

However, I listened to the voice of God and told the lady what to do. I told her to believe God and she rejoiced for her healing. At the end of the service, she spoke to me and said that she believed God had commanded healing for her that day. Obedience to God is the key to prosperity in life.

**I beseech you therefore, brethren, by the mercies of God: trust and obey.**

A song sung in churches across the world tells us that there is no other way to be happy in Jesus than for us to trust and obey.

## Brawta Scripture

"You must love the LORD your God and obey all his requirements, decrees, regulations, and commands" (Deuteronomy 11:1, NLT).

## REFLECTION

Are you struggling with obedience?

_____

_____

_____

_____

_____

What ridiculous instruction has God given you that
you failed to obey?

_____

_____

_____

_____

_____

Is obedience a key in your Christian journey?

_____

_____

_____

_____

# Write to God

About building your level of obedience.

# Day 22
# POSITIONED IN WORSHIP

"Then King Jehoshaphat bowed low with his face
to the ground. And all the people of Judah and
Jerusalem did the same, worshiping the Lord"
(2 Chronicles 20:18, NLT).

## Encouragement

How many times have we heard that worship is a lifestyle? As cliché as it sounds, it is true. We are encouraged to live a life of worship. Worship and praise are two different things. Everything on the earth, the animals, the plants, and the universe can praise God, but only those washed in the blood of Christ can truly worship. Worship is from the heart. It comes from deep within and not just from our mouth. Worship is, therefore, a lifestyle that we must have at all times.

Out of obedience comes worship. Jehoshaphat followed the Lord's instructions, went to the mountain and watched the Lord fight the battle. In the midst of and even after that, the king and the people of Judah sang praises unto God for the battle had been won. Give God the praise for the battle you are in has been won. Your foe has been overcome. Give praise to the Father and glory to the Son. Let worship be your most sacred position. Let your life express your love for God. In everything you do, people should know that you are a worshipper because only true believers can worship.

## Testimony

Obedience invokes worship, and worship triggers the response of God. My lifestyle today has been heavily positioned in worship. If I get bad news, I worship, and if the news is good, I worship just the same. I had no money to fly out to a conference but my ticket was already purchased. I was worried at first until I reassured myself that God would deal with it. I worshipped God with my faith and trust. The night before my flight, my grandmother called me, and she and my mother gave me a little over US$200, and on my way to board the plane my travel partner and big brother in the ministry said that my associate pastor gave him money to give me. Upon my arrival in America, I had over US$300, and by the time I got to St. Kitts, I had near US$290.

Upon leaving the conference, someone came to me and said, "I just felt led to give you US$50." I ended up leaving St. Kitts with the same amount of money with which I went. I worshipped God in the state of not having money. His instructions were for me to go to the conference and not worry. My National Overseer took care of the room at the hotel, and everything was paid for. My lifestyle is worship, and I hope your position is or will be the same.

**I beseech you therefore, brethren, by the mercies of God: Let worship be your lifestyle.**

Worship must not be seasonal but continual. Let your position of worship be a daily thing.

## Brawta

"Exalt the Lord our God, and worship at his holy mountain in Jerusalem, for the Lord our God is holy!"
(Psalm 99:9, NLT)

# REFLECTION

What is your definition of worship?

_____

_____

_____

_____

_____

What do you think living a life of worship means?

_____

_____

_____

_____

_____

_____

What Scripture comes to mind when you hear the word worship?

_____

_____

_____

_____

_____

## Write to God

About living a life of worship.

_____

_____

_____

_____

# Day 23
# BROKEN CRAYONS STILL COLOUR

"Purify me from my sins, and I will be clean; wash
me, and I will be whiter than snow"
(Psalm 51:7, NLT).

## Encouragement

If we are honest with ourselves, we would know that there are times when we commit sins that we planned and sometimes sins that are unplanned. There are times we become broken down after we have committed a crime against God, and feel as if we have no right and part with God or the things of God. The feelings of uselessness sometimes overtake us after we have sinned. Be honest with yourself us—from the time of your salvation until now us—you have sinned at some point, and experienced the feeling of regret. You feel regret for the things you have done, and the acts you have committed against God. We all have been there, and maybe today, you are there.

Maybe you have sinned and feel as if you are unworthy to take part in the things of God. King David committed a sin and slept with a man's wife, killed her husband, and tried to cover it up. He had sinned big time, but yet God called him a man after His (God) own heart. This interesting story tells me, and I hope it tells you too, that broken crayons still colour. Though we have sinned against God, we need to repent because we still have use in His kingdom. Whatever sins you have committed, repent and continue to colour the pages of your life with the words of God. You might have sinned and become broken but you are not useless. Repent and colour. Sometimes persons have hurt you and caused you to be broken, in this regard, forgive and colour.

## Testimony

I remember one year in my Christian journey, I felt as if I had no use. Yes, I could still preach and I led worship from the heart but I messed up and sinned against

God. Someone I looked up to hurt me with cruel words and that put my life into a downward spiral. I said some things that were not becoming of a Christian, especially to a Senior Minister. I spoke words that hurt as I was hurt and I resorted to high levels of sarcasm. For one year, I did not care about the feelings of others. I felt as if I was not worthy to come before His people to say or do anything. I do not grade sin as bigger or lesser. In my eyes, sin is sin. For almost one year, I was in and out of depression because I felt as if my broken state was never going to be mended. Out of hurt, I hurt others. I prayed and asked God to forgive me and I repented.

In that very same year, the Lord sent a word to me at an event where I was the master of ceremony; the word was an encouragement to tell me that I should not live in my past or in pity, but rise up to where God was taking me, for He had forgiven me. To this very day, I have it in my mind; no matter how I sin against God, He still loves me. And if I'm honest in my repentance, I can colour again. As broken as I was, I was reminded that broken crayons still colour. Today, I try my best to be respectful of people's feeling; for if I want to colour the world with the word of God, I must first colour my life with it. I was broken, and sometimes I still feel broken but broken crayons colour just as well as whole crayons. Never feel useless, colour with the grace of God.

**I beseech you therefore, brethren, by the mercies of God: Do not stop colouring because you were once broken.**

The state of brokenness is not permanent, repent and colour, then watch how God will make the broken part of your life become whole again. You may be broken, but you still have use. You can still colour.

## Brawta Scripture

Just then his disciples came back. They were shocked to find him talking to a woman, but none of them had the nerve to ask, "What do you want with her?" or "Why are you talking to her?" The woman left her water jar beside the well and ran back to the village, telling everyone, "Come and see a man who told me everything I ever did! Could he possibly be the Messiah?" So, the people came streaming from the village to see him (John 4:27-30, NLT).

# REFLECTION

What area of your life are you having challenges with?

_____

_____

_____

_____

_____

_____

What brokenness have you experienced?

_____

_____

_____

_____

_____

_____

Do you see yourself as useful?

_____

_____

_____

_____

_____

_____

## Write to God

Ask Him to mend your broken ways so that you can colour the world with his word.

_____

_____

_____

_____

# Day 24
## BREAK THE TIES

"And if your right hand causes you to sin, cut it off
and throw it away. For it is better that you lose one
of your members than that your whole body goes
into hell" (Matthew 5:30, ESV).

## Encouragement

It is always easier to say something than to do it. If
we are true to ourselves, we have said that we
were going to do things more than once but honestly, we have yet to do it. This is because saying it is
much easier than doing it. However, doing it, is much
more beneficial to us. How many times have you said,
"I'm going to stop going there" or "I am going to stop
talking to that person?" Truly some things, some places and some people are really bad for us, and because
we have encountered them repeatedly, we have devel-

oped a strong tie or an addiction to these places, people and things.

For those who have been in sexual activities, a soul tie may have been formed. Those who have been to parties and have been exposed to pornography or excessive drinking of alcohol and smoking herbs may also encounter addiction. At some point, all of us have encountered a pull or an attraction to something that was not good for us. Look into your life and identify the thing, person or place that has not been good for you but you find yourself attached to it or them.

You do not have to be tied up any longer. Jesus has come to set you free, and today we are breaking every single tie. Today, through the power of the Holy Spirit, we are going to dismantle every chain and today, freedom is coming. We are breaking the ties that bind us to unfruitful lifestyles; the ties that bind us to poverty; the ties that bind us to lasciviousness and the ties that hold us down.

Day 24 is practical; therefore, we should not just read, but we should act.

## Testimony

I made a very big decision in 2019. As with many of the hard decisions I had to make, I tend to over think. I had to cut off communications with some people. They were not beneficial to my spiritual growth. Although they were cool and calm in their own way, they were not impacting my life the way I would want them to. I decided that to break ties because of where God is taking me. It was difficult because I had built such a strong bond with one that I tried to rationalize how we could remain friends but limit communication.

The Lord then revealed to me on three levels why I needed to break the bond. 1). Psychologically, it was not healthy 2) spiritually it was detrimental and 3) emotionally, it would have been damaging. It was a friendship that was toxic but I did not see it until months later. I decided I had to be bold and end it.

Today, I stand free from that individual, and we have no animosity towards each other as we both understood the reason for the decision. You will be the better you when you decide to break the ties that are holding you down.

**I beseech you, therefore, brethren, by the mercies of God: Cut off all unhealthy ties.**

Learn to discern what is right for you and when you find out that something is not healthy, cut it off. And when you cut it/them off, do not go back to them/it!

## Brawta Scripture

"For freedom Christ has set us free; stand firm therefore, and do not submit again to a yoke of slavery" (Galatians 5:1).

# REFLECTION

What/who have you been tied to that you need to cut off?

_____

_____

_____

_____

_____

What's your understanding of soul ties?

_____

_____

_____

_____

_____

_____

Do you find it hard to break the ties to people, things and places?

_____

_____

_____

_____

_____

In this segment I invite you to pray this prayer with me:

## Let's Pray to God

*Father in Heaven, I come to you knowing that you are just and able to forgive us of our sins. I ask that you blot out my transgression and break every tie that is unhealthy in my life. I ask that you clean my mind, heart and spirit from everything that is against your will that has attached itself to me. I declare that every chain is broken and every tie destroyed. Friends that are unhealthy will walk away from my life without even saying goodbye. Things that are unhealthy will become unappealing to me, and places that are unholy will become repulsive to my spiritual man. I declare that I am free today from all ties, in Jesus name. Amen.*

## Write to God

Tell Him from what you need to be freed.

_____

_____

_____

_____

_____

_____

# Day 25
# GO GET YOUR LIFE BACK

To illustrate the point further, Jesus told them this story: A man had two sons. The younger son told his father, 'I want my share of your estate now before you die.' So, his father agreed to divide his wealth between his sons. A few days later this younger son packed all his belongings and moved to a distant land, and there he wasted all his money in wild living.

About the time his money ran out, a great famine swept over the land, and he began to starve. He persuaded a local farmer to hire him, and the man sent him into his fields to feed the pigs. The young man became so hungry that even the pods he was feeding the pigs looked good to him. But no one gave him anything.

When he finally came to his senses, he said to himself, 'At home, even the hired servants have food enough to spare, and here I am dying of hunger! I will go home to my father and say, 'Father, I have sinned against both heaven and you, and I am no longer worthy of being called your son. Please take me on as a hired servant.'

So he returned home to his father. And while he was still a long way off, his father saw him coming. Filled with love and compassion, he ran to his son, embraced him, and kissed him. His son said to him, 'Father, I have sinned against both heaven and you, and I am no longer worthy of being called your son.'

But his father said to the servants, 'Quick! Bring the finest robe in the house and put it on him. Get a ring for his finger and sandals for his feet. And kill the calf we have been fattening. We must celebrate with a feast, for this son of mine was dead and has now returned to life. He was lost, but now he is found.' So the party began.

Meanwhile, the older son was in the fields working. When he returned home, he heard music and dancing in the house, and he asked one of the servants what was going on. 'Your brother is back,' he was told, 'and your father has killed the fattened calf. We are celebrating because of his safe return.' The older brother was angry and wouldn't go in. His father came out and begged him, but he replied, 'All these years I've slaved for you and never once refused to do a single thing you told me to. And in all that time you never gave me even one young goat for a feast with my friends. Yet when this son of yours comes back after squandering your money on prostitutes, you celebrate by killing the fattened calf!'

His father said to him, 'Look, dear son, you have always stayed by me, and everything I have is yours. We had to celebrate this happy day. For your brother was dead and has come back to life! He was lost, but now he is found!' (Luke 15:11-32, NIV).

## Encouragement

We have all made mistakes in life, and like the prodigal son, we have walked away from our royal lifestyle to explore the impurities of the world. Truly Christianity is not easy, and at times we encounter this spirit called pride that pushes us to "want to spend our inheritance." Sometimes pride pushes us into the pig pens of life, causing us to eat among the creatures of the earth that we were set above to rule.

Interestingly, the prodigal son came to his senses to get his life back, but what stood out in the text was how his father was expecting him, waiting to embrace him with love and enfold him back into his rightful place. Though you have walked away, messed up, may have been in some pig pens, you are encouraged today to get your life back. God represents the father in the story. He is expecting you to return so that He can embrace you with love and restore you to your rightful place.

## Testimony

The testimony here is that of Luke 15:11-32. We have read it, and in summary, this is what it says. The younger son decided to take his inheritance and squander it. After encountering the hardship, he made a decision to return to his father's house as a servant. On his way home his father met him and embraced him and welcomed him home with a big party. Though his initial decision was foolish, his ultimate decision to try and get his life back on track, restored him to his royal position. You have made decisions like the prodigal son, but you are now encouraged to get your life back.

**I beseech you therefore, brethren, by the mercies of God: Get Your Life Back.**

Things will happen and some decisions you make will be foolish, but brush off yourself, get up and go get your life back! Be who God has called you to be!

## Brawta Scripture

"Come, let us return to the LORD. He has torn us to pieces; now he will heal us. He has injured us; now he will bandage our wounds" (Hosea 6:1, NLT).

# REFLECTION

What are the steps you need to take to get your life back on track?

_____

_____

_____

_____

_____

_____

_____

_____

What caused you to wander from your true calling?

_____

_____

_____

_____

_____

_____

_____

_____

Are you ready to get your life back?

_____

_____

_____

_____

_____

_____

# Write to God

Express your desire to regain your true identity in Him.

---

---

---

---

---

---

---

---

---

---

---

---

---

---

---

# Day 26
# SEASONS CHANGE BUT GOD IS CONSTANT

"Then he will send the rains in their proper sea-
sons--the early and late rains--so you can bring in
your harvests of grain, new wine, and olive oil"
(Deuteronomy 11:14, NLT).

## Encouragement

The wise man Solomon tells us that there is a time and a season for everything under the sun. I do agree with this saying. We all have seasons in our lives. Some seasons are hard to talk about because they may have been seasons of tests and trials. You may have encountered seasons of heavy rains and floods; seasons of turmoil and possibly seasons of loss. For everything, there is a season. There is a time when we laugh and a time when we cry. We may not be able to predict the season, but one thing I can assure you is that while seasons change, God remains the same. Though we cannot predict our seasons, we can definitely live through them.

In every rainy season, God is a shelter for us. In every dry season, God has a brook filled with water waiting for us. He is the water of life, the living water. In every sad season, God is our comforter. In every dark and gloomy season, God is our light and guide

Do not watch the changes of life around you, but keep your focus on the one who does not change. In the seasons of life, there is always good because there will always be God. As the Scripture says, God will send what you need in due time. Your season is now, walk into it, it's your good season because God is with you.

## Testimony

Seasons change, but God is constant. I never thought in my wildest dreams that I would be doing so much in church. It was prophesied, but the season in which the prophecy came, caused me to doubt the prophecy because the season said otherwise. I finally believed the prophetic word and stepped out on it. I preached my first sermon on a Sabbath afternoon, and since that time, I've become an itinerant preacher. My season changed, but the word of God was not going to change with the seasons of life. The Lord, through a sermon preached by Bishop Noel Jones, whom I greatly admire, spoke clearly to me saying: "I will make your name great."

I have preached in multiple denominations, before great preachers of this age and time without holding a decorative ecclesiastical position. My name is broadcasted across Jamaica and the world daily, and often I remember the word the Lord gave me. Today, I can say seasons change but God and His word remain constant. Whatever season you are in, it is your good season because God is in it with you.

**I beseech you therefore, brethren, by the mercies of God: Walk into your good season**.

With the ever-changing times remember that God is never changing and no matter the turmoil around you, the season you are in now serves a purpose- walk into your good season trusting the God who is constant.

## Brawta Scripture

"Jesus Christ is the same yesterday, today, and forever" (Hebrews 13:8, NLT).

# REFLECTION

How has God proven himself as constant to you?

_____

_____

_____

_____

_____

Seasons change, but God is constant. What does that mean to you?

_____

_____

_____

_____

_____

_____

Name one attribute of God that stood out to you in your worst season of life.

_____

_____

_____

_____

_____

_____

_____

# Write to God

Based on the season you are in, write your heart's deepest cry to God.

_____

_____

_____

_____

_____

_____

_____

_____

_____

_____

_____

_____

_____

# Day 27
## NEW MERCIES

"The faithful love of the Lord never ends!
His mercies never cease. Great is his faithfulness;
his mercies begin afresh each morning"
(Lamentations 3:22-23, NLT).

## Encouragement

With a new day comes new mercies. Honestly, we could have been consumed by the worries of the days gone by, but the Lord rewards us each day with mercies. Not just mercies, but brand-new mercies. It shows us that God gives us what we do not deserve. When God bestows mercy unto us is, it's His way that He has withheld the wrath and judgment we deserve.

We are undeserving of His unfailing love and mercies but each morning that we open our eyes we experience brand new mercies. We get the smell of the fresh air and see the sunlight which we often take for granted. We have been given another chance on this earth to worship the Creator. God's mercies never cease, and God's faithfulness is greater than we can imagine. Each day you breathe, be encouraged that God loves you so much that He withheld His wrath and has given you brand new mercies.

## Testimony

I recall one night when my body was in agonizing pain that I cried myself to sleep. Later, I woke up in the night still crying. I felt as if I was not going to make it till daybreak. I was sure I was going to die. I immediately repented of any and every sin. Even if I had done nothing wrong, I still went to God and asked for forgiveness because the pain was so intense. At about 4 a.m. I was finally able to sleep. My lullaby was the old hymn: *Christ Returneth* and I woke up singing *Great is thy faithfulness* and I was in far less pain and much more strength. I woke up to healing and new mercies. God has withheld His wrath from us even though we deserve it, and He has given us new mercies.

**I beseech you therefore, brethren, by the mercies of God: thank God for new mercies.**

Never feel as if you are entitled to the mercies of God but always be humble enough to exalt Him for the new mercies bestowed upon you.

## Brawta Scripture

"But you, O Lord, are a God of compassion and mercy, slow to get angry and filled with unfailing love and faithfulness"
(Psalm 86:15, NLT).

# REFLECTION

What mercies are you thankful for?

_____

_____

_____

_____

_____

When was the last time you thanked God for His new mercies towards you?

_____

_____

_____

_____

_____

_____

_____

How do you feel knowing that God loves you enough to withhold wrath and instead extends mercy to you?

_____

_____

_____

_____

_____

_____

## Write to God

A prayer of thanksgiving for His new mercies.

_____

_____

_____

_____

_____

_____

_____

# Day 28
## SMILE AGAIN

"A cheerful look brings joy to the heart; good news makes for good health" (Proverbs 15:30, NLT).

## Encouragement

Growing up, I have always heard that frowning requires us to use more facial muscles than when we smile. When we smile, our muscles are more relaxed and not pressured. For some of us, smiling every minute is just not a part of our personality. To be honest, there are times when I am extremely happy but my face may not show it. You may be like me. Outside of that, there comes a point when you have to smile. Life can get depressing at times, and things can happen that may push us to frown and be gloomy.

When last did you smile in such a way that your lips spread from cheek to cheek touching near your ears? For some of us, the pressures of life have taken away our smile. We have become despondent, and our face reflects lost hope. I encourage you to smile again because it will bring joy to the heart. Even if things look bleak and catastrophic, smile. Do not let anything or anyone steal your happiness. Smile in the face of the hurt and live your life. Smile again. No more frowning for the greater One is in you.

## Testimony

Smiling makes a big difference in life. I received some bad news once, and it was devastating because it related to financial stability. Without divulging much information, someone who knew of the situation asked me, "Why are you smiling, aren't you worried?" My immediate response was, "What else can I do but smile?" I have learnt in life that things will not always go the way you expect, but even when things do not go your way, smile no matter what. Confuse the enemy with your smile. Have him wonder why you are happy in the midst of chaos. To date, I am smiling even as I type this and I smile because I know God is working things out for me. I believe He is working things out for you too, so smile again. Give your face a rest.

**I beseech you therefore, brethren, by the mercies of God: Smile again and rest your face.**

Do not let the cares of life take away your smile. Smile in the midst of the storm; smile when things are going well, and smile when things don't seem to be working in your favour. Smile just because you know God is working behind the scenes for you. A famous singer exhorts us in her song "...and He's working it out for you."

## Brawta Scripture

"We were filled with laughter, and we sang for joy. And the other nations said, 'What amazing things the LORD has done for them' (Psalm 126:2, NLT).

# REFLECTION

What has God done for you that brought a smile to your face?

_____

_____

_____

_____

_____

_____

When last have you given a genuine smile?

_____

_____

_____

_____

_____

# Write to God

Remind God of the time He made you smile.

_____

_____

_____

_____

_____

_____

_____

_____

_____

_____

_____

_____

_____

_____

# Day 29
# YOU ARE AN HEIR

"And now that you belong to Christ, you are the true children of Abraham. You are his heirs, and God's promise to Abraham belongs to you" (Galatians 3:29, NLT).

## Encouragement

You are royalty! Let that sink in for a while. Stop living like a peasant. God has called us heirs to His Kingdom. You are important. You have power in Christ Jesus. God has extended to you a benefit that only His sons and daughters can have. Why are you acting as if you are worth any less? You are more than you think you are. You were selected to be a part of the royal priesthood. You were carved out to be a holy nation. Peculiarity is in your

DNA and holiness should be your lifestyle. Today, I encourage you: *act like royalty.*

## Testimony

I was driving home from a meeting and I stopped at a stoplight. As I stopped, I noticed a young man approaching my car. I started to roll up the window as a safety precaution, but while doing so, I felt the nudge to hand him all the money that was in the side of the door. It was not a lot, but it sufficed that evening. He looked at me and respectfully said thanks. I felt good on the inside. Even though I needed the money myself, God reminded me that I was an heir and therefore, the promises of my forefathers were also mine and the things of the kingdom belonged to me.

With that in mind, I gave freely because the royal priesthood must be able to help others. The Lord reminded me that it was the very same day that I had no money but I dressed as if I had all the money in the world, that I received five thousand dollars (J$5000.00) in hand to perform a simple task. As heirs to the kingdom, the King, our Father, will always take care of you and me.

**I beseech you therefore, brethren, by the mercies of God: Act like royalty.**

Even though you are royalty, do not pretend to be better than anyone but help everyone that you can help. Treat them in the same manner as you would want to be treated. Remember the golden rule: D*o unto others as you would have them do unto you.*

## Brawta Scripture

"Now you are no longer a slave but God's own child. And since you are his child, God has made you his heir" (Galatians 4:7, NLT).

# REFLECTION

Do you see yourself as an heir to the kingdom?

_____

_____

_____

_____

_____

What priestly duties have you done?

_____

_____

_____

_____

_____

_____

How has your life reflected that of a member of the royal priesthood, holy nation and a peculiar people?

_____

_____

_____

_____

_____

## Write to God

Ask Him to show you how to walk into your rightful calling.

_____

_____

_____

_____

_____

_____

_____

# Day 30
# TAKE THE LIMITS OFF

"I am the Lord, the God of all the peoples of the world. Is anything too hard for me?" (Jeremiah 32:27, NLT).

## Encouragement

Welcome to the final day of this encouragement guide. Today is simple. I just want to encourage you to take the limits off. Take the limits from off your life and more so, take the limits off God. Sometimes life can be hard. Things will not play out the way you want and sometimes the impossibilities are before your eyes and you are stuck. Some people get stuck at a place of worry; a place of sadness and sometimes a place of inconsistency.

Today is your day to take off the limits. The reason why you have not yet excelled as you should might be because you have limited yourself from accomplishing certain tasks, or you may have placed limits on God, believing that He cannot do what you would want Him to do for you. In our human nature, it is easier to fall into despair and feel as if life is not working in our favour. We tend to limit ourselves in our minds. Our biggest enemy is not the devil, but our biggest enemy is ourselves. Until we learn to deal with ourselves, we will always limit our faith, our trust and our hope in God. You are encouraged to remove the limit from your mind. Remove the limit you have placed on God because there is nothing too hard for Him to do. Remember He can do exceeding and abundantly more than you could ask or imagine. What limits have you placed on your life? I implore you, take the limits off.

## Testimony

My mantra, "Whatever you do, do it to the best of your ability," helps me every day along with my closing words on air, "Love yourself, you're your neighbour as yourself but most importantly, love God the most.

Walk good." My older brother Kaswayne Budhan has been someone I admire as it relates to educational goals. He passed 19 subjects in CXC and CAPE. He speaks fluent Spanish and is always ready to learn something new.

Not many persons believed that I would be as brilliant as my brother, and they placed limits on my educational achievements. However, I had close family and friends who encouraged me to push pass the limits that others placed on my life. I was scared to share my CXC results with others because it was not as much as what my older brother achieved. I started to limit my own educational growth believing that I was not as good as I thought.

Nevertheless, my parents and grandparents believed in me. I went to HEART Trust and completed a two-year certificate course within eleven months. I wanted to be a chef at that time. After completing the certificate course, I enrolled at Jamaica Theological Seminary and completed a four-year Bachelor of Arts degree in Theology and Guidance and Counselling. I removed the limits. I started to think big. I applied to Gordon-Conwell Theological Seminary in Boston and got accepted to do a Master of Divinity.

Due to financial reasons I opted to study in Jamaica. With the limits were removed, God started opening doors. My courses were paid for and I was asked to speak at multiple events. While doing the master's degree, I completed a diploma in Christian Leadership from the New Covenant Bible Institute. I also completed studies in Business Process Outsourcing (BPO) and Customer Service. I think I mentioned this before in other chapters. Where did I get the time to do all of this? That's a good question that I ask myself. I told the Lord that I want to be great and I will never limit Him and what He can do in my life. I am a limitless believer of Christ. Whatever you are doing, be great at doing it and make sure it is pleasing to God.

**I beseech you therefore, brethren, by the mercies of God: Take the limits off.**

Do not let life scare you. Rough patches will come, but you have to be limitless if you are serving a God who cannot be controlled by time, space or matter. Take the limits off God and He will cause you to soar higher than you would have ever imagined.

## Brawta Scripture

"God can do anything you know, far more than you could ever imagine or guess or request in your wildest dreams! He does it not by pushing us around but by working within us, his Spirit deeply and gently within us" (Eph. 3:20, MSG).

# REFLECTION

In this reflection, write your heart to God and think hard on your responses to the questions.

What limitations have you placed on yourself?

_____

_____

_____

_____

_____

_____

_____

_____

Do you believe that God can do greater than what you image?

_____

_____

_____

_____

_____

_____

Are you ready to remove those limits and soar higher in God?

_____

_____

_____

_____

_____

_____

_____

_____

_____

_____

_____

## Write to God

Write the "impossibilities" that you expect to see happen in your life for this year and years to come! Take the limits off and WRITE.

_____

_____

_____

_____

_____

_____

# PREPARATION

"But He knows where I am going. And when He
tests me, I will come out as pure gold" (Job 23:10,
NLT)"

T hings happen in your life to perfect you and to
make you into the pure gold that God has created you to be. God does not tempt, but He
tests. He tests to see if you will stay with him when
you feel His presence and when you feel as if He has
left you alone. God evades our sensuality to build our
trust in Him. He knows the route you must take to be
the best you and He will always do His best to refine
you so that when the test is over, you shall be as pure
gold. Here is my prayer for you.

# My Prayer for You

Father, I come to you in the name of Jesus Christ, our Lord and Saviour. I present the reader before you. You know them by name and by nature. You are sovereign over their lives and you are the protector for the future days to come. I ask that you will strengthen them in the trials of life come their way. I pray God that you will remind them that you are on the journey with them, and you indeed know the way they should take.

Remove all the limits put on them and in their lives. I prophesy that they will soar to new heights and new dimensions in you. I stand against the spirit of fear and frustration. I stand against the spirit of intimidation that has been plaguing them night and day. I pray that they will no longer live in a state of regret but in state of progress. I pray that they will prosper in all they do that God will open windows of blessings from heaven over their lives. I pray their lives will never be the same again. I pray that testimonies will come from them that will encourage others. I commit their plans to you and praise you for what you are doing in their lives now, in Jesus' name, Amen.

# Pray with Me

Father, thank you for your many blessings bestowed upon me. Thank you for your gifts given to enhance my life. Thank you for the calling upon my life. Thank you for the purpose birthed within me. Thank you for the new mercies granted to me each morning. Thank you for your love towards me. Thank you for covering me, shielding me from the enemy and protecting me from myself. Father, I pray in the name of Jesus that I shall not be less than what you have called me to be but I shall walk in a greater calling, greater anointing and into a greater relationship with you, without any limits, in Jesus name. Amen.

# PREPARATION

"But He knows where I am going. And when He tests me, I will come out as pure gold" (Job 23:10, NLT)"

Things happen in your life to perfect you and to make you into the pure gold that God has created you to be. God does not tempt, but He tests. He tests to see if you will stay with him when you feel His presence and when you feel as if He has left you alone. God evades our sensuality to build our trust in Him. He knows the route you must take to be the best you and He will always do His best to refine you so that when the test is over, you shall be as pure gold. Here is my prayer for you.

# My Prayer for You

Father, I come to you in the name of Jesus Christ, our Lord and Saviour. I present the reader before you. You know them by name and by nature. You are sovereign over their lives and you are the protector for the future days to come. I ask that you will strengthen them in the trials of life come their way. I pray God that you will remind them that you are on the journey with them, and you indeed know the way they should take.

Remove all the limits put on them and in their lives. I prophesy that they will soar to new heights and new dimensions in you. I stand against the spirit of fear and frustration. I stand against the spirit of intimidation that has been plaguing them night and day. I pray that they will no longer live in a state of regret but in state of progress. I pray that they will prosper in all they do that God will open windows of blessings from heaven over their lives. I pray their lives will never be the same again. I pray that testimonies will come from them that will encourage others. I commit their plans to you and praise you for what you are doing in their lives now, in Jesus' name, Amen.

# ACKNOWLEDGEMENTS

I thank God for the knowledge, wisdom and persistence in completing this book. My family plays an integral role in my life and has contributed greatly to my growth and development. I want to extend love and blessings to my parents, Murphy and Raffie Budhan, and my grandmother, Grace Bromfield, for always reminding me how proud they are of me.

Thank you to my editor Carlene Dacres and my proofreaders: Amanda Cooke, Shanice Senior and Richard Robinson for ensuring the book is error free.

Thanks to you, readers, for taking the time out to purchase and read this book.

# UPCOMING BOOK

Overcoming an addiction is not easy at all. Overcoming personal struggles faced during life on earth is a challenging task, but with God, we can overcome all things. In this riveting discourse, the book *Overcoming* looks at some common issues that humans face in life and applies biblical principles to overcoming those issues. Not only does *Overcoming* provide a Biblical foundation for overcoming these issues, but it also includes psychological and sociological perspectives to transform readers from being under the weather to overcoming the debris blown at them.

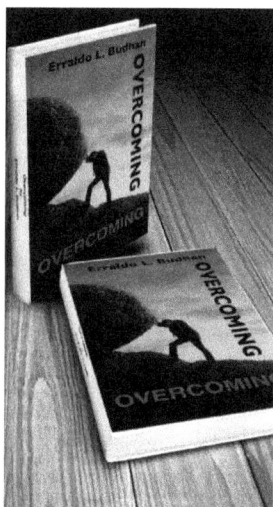

We will look at overcoming different aspects of **FEAR,** and what I consider to be the demon of **PROCRASTINATION**.

Do you procrastinate often? Well, the Bible has an answer for everything, and in **Overcoming** we will explore the biblical tenets of how we overcome procrastination and many more issues. Interesting reflections, transformational activities and more await you when you get the book: ***Overcoming.*** It will assist you in transforming your life to experience the life God wants you to have.

> "I have told you these things, so that in me you may have peace. In this world you will have trouble. But take heart! I have overcome the world" (John 16:33, NIV).

# ABOUT THE AUTHOR

Lay Minister Erraldo Budhan holds a Bachelor of Arts Degree in Theology at the Jamaica Theological Seminary. He is currently enrolled at the Caribbean Graduate School of Theology where he is pursuing a Master of Arts in Theological Studies. Erraldo also holds a Diploma in Christian Leadership from the New Covenant Bible Institute.

He has completed a Master Trainer workshop with the Ministry of Education Youth and Information which certifies him to train persons in understanding the Business Process Outsourcing (B.P.O.) industry and customer service. He is a trained Guidance Counsellor currently working at St. Michael's Primary, and also a Radio Announcer with Love101 FM.

He has been a Christian for over ten years and has no regrets about his decision to serve the Lord Jesus Christ. He currently worships at the Life Centre Tabernacle Church of God of Prophecy. He has been appointed to the office of Parish Youth and Young Adult Ministry Director for the Church of God of Prophecy St. Catherine East.

Erraldo serves as a Board Director with Operation Youth Reap Ltd. Erraldo and as a member of the National Convention Planning Committee and National Public Relations Committee of the Church of God of Prophecy, Jamaica.

He strongly believes that the Lord has called him into an apostolic leadership and has confirmed such calling through numerous prophetic words. With such a calling on his life, his aim is to cultivate young leaders to develop their gifts and find their purpose in ministry.